THINGS THAT GO!

ADAM HARRIS

WELCOME!

IN THIS BOOK,
YOU WILL NEED TO
MATCH THE CORRECT
LETTER WITH THE
RIGHT VEHICLE.

ARE YOU READY?
GOOD LUCK!

I SPY WITH MY LITTLE EYE, SOMETHING BEGINNING WITH...

A IS FOR AMBULANCE!

I SPY WITH MY LITTLE EYE, SOMETHING BEGINNING WITH...

 **IS FOR** B**IPLANE!**

I SPY WITH MY LITTLE EYE, SOMETHING BEGINNING WITH...

C IS FOR CONCRETE MIXER TRUCK!

I SPY WITH MY LITTLE EYE, SOMETHING BEGINNING WITH...

 **IS FOR DUMP TRUCK!**

I SPY WITH MY LITTLE EYE, SOMETHING BEGINNING WITH...

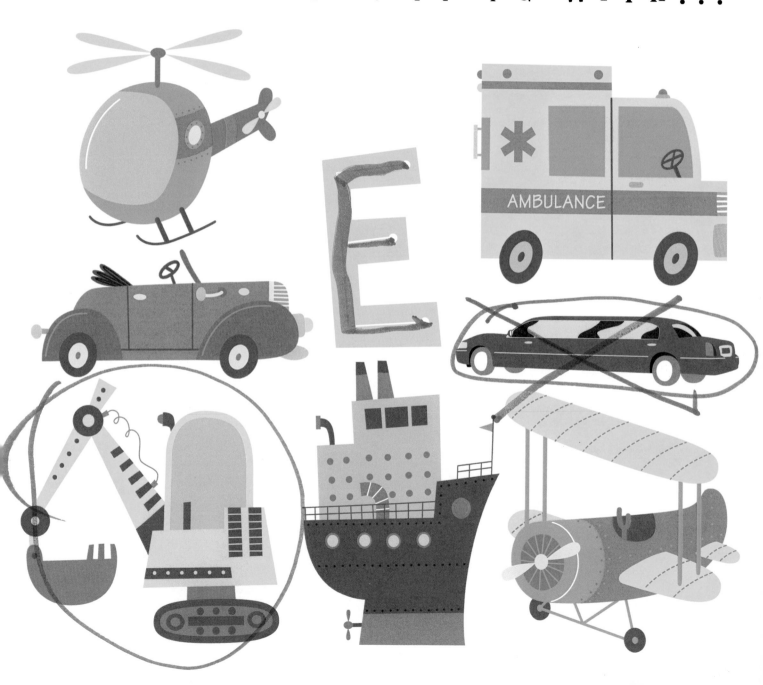

E IS FOR EXCAVATOR!

I SPY WITH MY LITTLE EYE, SOMETHING BEGINNING WITH...

F IS FOR FIRE TRUCK!

I SPY WITH MY LITTLE EYE, SOMETHING BEGINNING WITH...

 **IS FOR GRADER!**

I SPY WITH MY LITTLE EYE, SOMETHING BEGINNING WITH...

H IS FOR HELICOPTER!

I SPY WITH MY LITTLE EYE, SOMETHING BEGINNING WITH...

IS FOR ICEBREAKER!

I SPY WITH MY LITTLE EYE, SOMETHING BEGINNING WITH...

J IS FOR JEEP!

I SPY WITH MY LITTLE EYE, SOMETHING BEGINNING WITH...

K IS FOR KAYAK!

I SPY WITH MY LITTLE EYE, SOMETHING BEGINNING WITH...

L IS FOR LIMOUSINE!

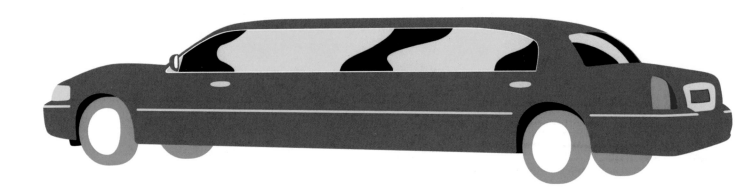

I SPY WITH MY LITTLE EYE, SOMETHING BEGINNING WITH...

M IS FOR MOTORCYCLE!

I SPY WITH MY LITTLE EYE, SOMETHING BEGINNING WITH...

IS FOR
NARROWBOAT!

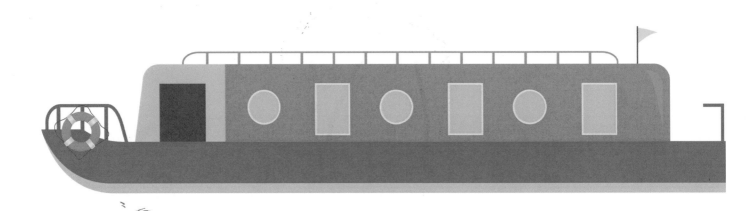

I SPY WITH MY LITTLE EYE, SOMETHING BEGINNING WITH...

 IS FOR OCEAN
LINER!

I SPY WITH MY LITTLE EYE, SOMETHING BEGINNING WITH...

 IS FOR POLICE CAR!

I SPY WITH MY LITTLE EYE, SOMETHING BEGINNING WITH...

Q IS FOR QUAD BIKE!

I SPY WITH MY LITTLE EYE, SOMETHING BEGINNING WITH...

 **IS FOR ROADSTER!**

I SPY WITH MY LITTLE EYE, SOMETHING BEGINNING WITH...

S IS FOR SUBMARINE!

I SPY WITH MY LITTLE EYE, SOMETHING BEGINNING WITH...

T IS FOR TANDEM BIKE!

I SPY WITH MY LITTLE EYE, SOMETHING BEGINNING WITH...

 IS FOR UNICYCLE!

I SPY WITH MY LITTLE EYE, SOMETHING BEGINNING WITH...

V IS FOR VAN!

I SPY WITH MY LITTLE EYE, SOMETHING BEGINNING WITH...

W IS FOR WHEELBARROW!

I SPY WITH MY LITTLE EYE, SOMETHING BEGINNING WITH...

 **IS FOR XEBEC!**

I SPY WITH MY LITTLE EYE, SOMETHING BEGINNING WITH...

Y IS FOR YACHT!

I SPY WITH MY LITTLE EYE, SOMETHING BEGINNING WITH...

 **IS FOR ZEPPELIN!**

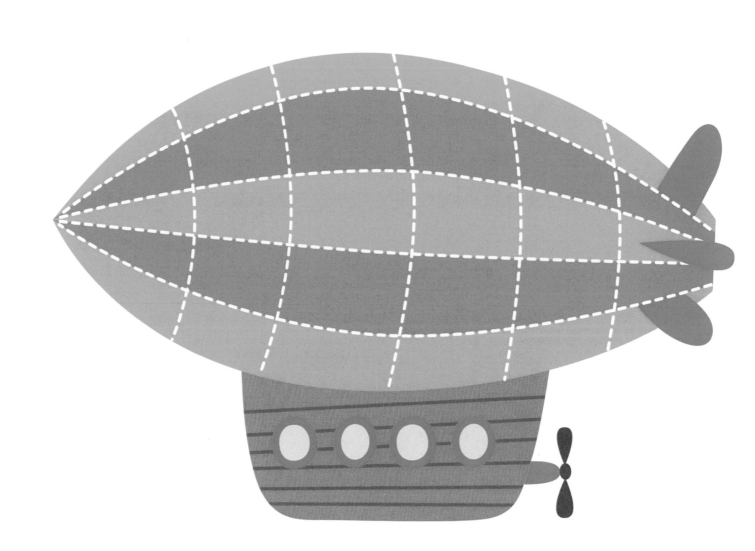

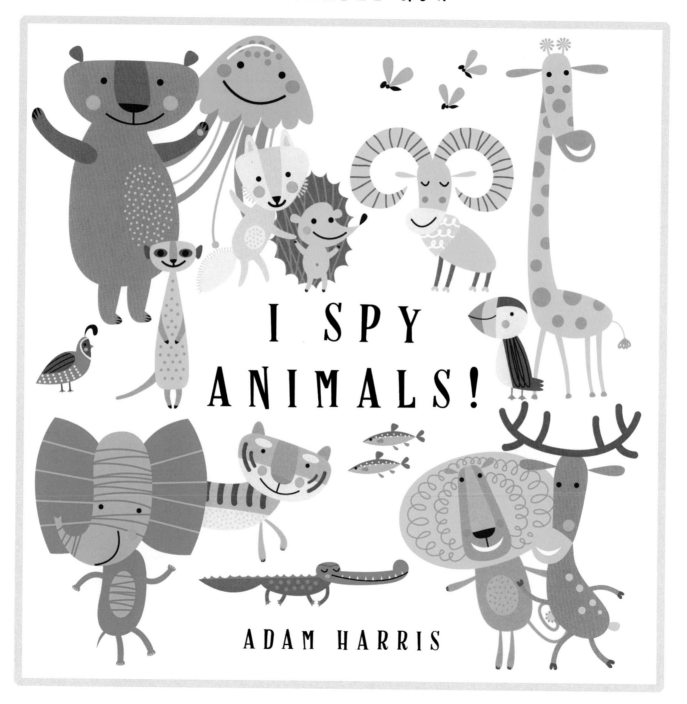

I SPY
ANIMALS!

ADAM HARRIS

PAPERBACK ISBN 978-0991736874
HARDCOVER ISBN 978-1999461508

ALSO AVAILABLE FROM

Young
DREAMERS
PRESS

Merry
Christmas

a black and white baby book

ADAM HARRIS

PAPERBACK ISBN 978-1999461515
HARDCOVER ISBN 978-1999461522